A Book About Sea Turtles
AMAZING EARTH: Wild Animal Facts
Written and designed by Dawon Seashore

Dawon Seashore
A Book
About
Sea Turtles
FOR KIDS

Dear reader,

We are happy to present to you A Book About Sea Turtles. This book is part of our Wild Animal Facts series where we take a look at some amazing facts about Earth's many fascinating animals.

The book was created for all youngsters out there, and any curious adult, who love to learn more about their favorite creatures.

We sincerely hope you enjoy and have fun reading. After, you can find out if you learned something new in a fun quiz at the end of the book. There are lots of beautiful photos as well!

Be sure to leave a review to let us know how you liked the book. It helps a lot to improve and expand on future publications.

Sincerely yours,

Wild Animal facts Team

TABLE OF CONTENT

Sea (marine) turtles are a **SUPERFAMILY** of animals called Chelonioidea.

They are divided into two families:

Hard-shelled sea turtles (Cheloniidae) that have a bony top shell.

Leathery-shelled sea turtles (Dermochelyidae) that have a less bony shell covered with skin.

WHAT ARE THEY?

Sea turtles are reptiles* which means they are cold-blooded, lay eggs, and have scaly skin.

Sea turtles are turtles – animals that have a shell made from their ribs.

RIBS - bones around the chest that protect the heart and lungs

You may have heard of tortoises as well.
Tortoises, turtles.
What is the difference?

READ ON TO FIND OUT!

*if the words in **blue** are a bit hard for you to understand, look up what they mean in the glossary at page 41-42

Tortoises have more rounded shells and live only on land.

Tortoise

Turtles have thinner shells so they can more easily swim. They spend time in water AND on land. Sea turtles are "special" turtles that spend most of their time in water.

Sea turtle

!

<u>Remember</u>: ALL TORTOISES ARE TURTLES BUT NOT ALL TURTLES ARE TORTOISES.

Did you know?
Sea turtles are among the oldest surviving reptiles in the world. They have existed for more than **150 million years.** That is when dinosaurs walked the Earth!

SPECIES OF SEA TURTLES

There are seven existing species of sea turtles:

1. green sea turtle
2. loggerhead sea turtle
3. Kemp's ridley sea turtle
4. olive ridley sea turtle
5. hawksbill sea turtle
6. flatback sea turtle
7. leatherback sea turtle**

**The leatherback sea turtle is the only one that has a leathery shell. The other six all have a hard shell!

Green sea turtle

TYPE OF SHELL:
hard shell

HOW BIG ARE THEY?

The leatherback sea turtle is the largest sea turtle species. It is usually 6–9 feet (2–3 meters) long, 3–5 feet (1–1.5 meters) wide, and can weigh up to 1500 pounds (700 kilograms)!

Other sea turtle species are smaller, being mostly 2–4 feet (60–120 cm) long.

A large body size helps sea turtles travel large distances. It also protects them against large predators in the ocean, such as sharks.

WHAT DO THEY LOOK LIKE?

Unlike most other animals, female and male sea turtles look the same and are the same size.

You can easily recognize most sea turtles by their hard shell.

The front flippers are used to move the sea turtle through the water.

The back flippers are used to control the direction in which they move.

Unlike terrestrial turtles, sea turtles have flippers instead of feet that allow them to swim faster.

Their jaws are powerful and shaped like a bird's beak.

Like all turtles, sea turtles don't have teeth.

Sea turtles have a strong sense of smell that helps them search for food.

Did you know?

Hawksbill turtles are typically found on coral reefs which are home to their favorite food—sponges. The shape of the beak of these sea turtles helps them search small holes in coral reefs to find food.

WHERE DO THEY LIVE?

HABITAT - Most sea turtles can be found in ALL oceans except for the polar regions. They live in open water and near coasts, mainly in tropical and subtropical waters.

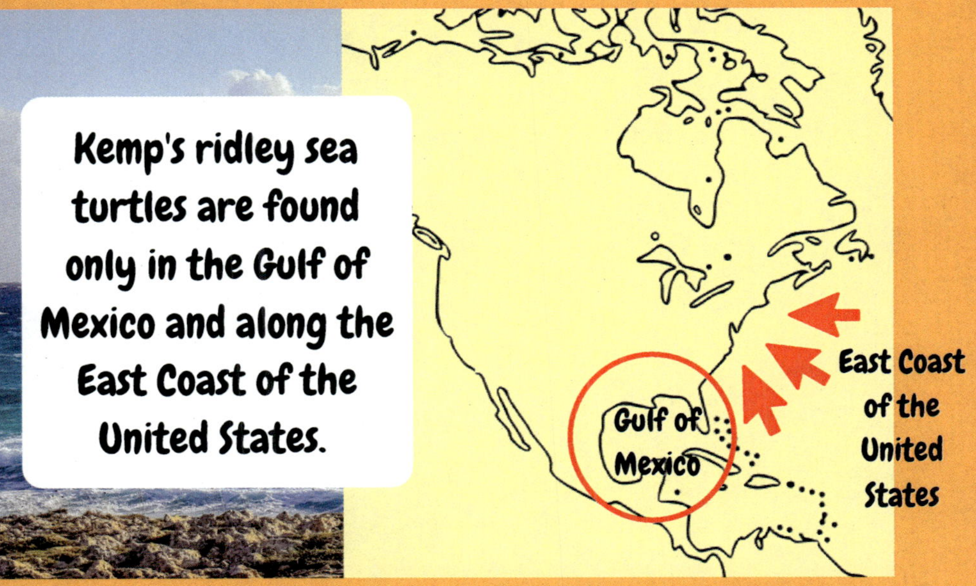

WHAT DO THEY EAT?

The loggerhead, Kemp's ridley, olive ridley, and hawksbill sea turtles are omnivores. They eat different plants and animals like seagrasses, seaweed, sponges, worms and fish.

Adult green sea turtles are herbivores.

Leatherback sea turtles eat almost only jellyfish.

Hawksbill sea turtles mainly eat sponges.

Did you know?

Green sea turtles are unique among sea turtles because they are herbivores, eating mostly seagrasses and algae. This diet gives their body fat (not the shells!) a greenish color which is where their name comes from.

COMMUNICATION

Sea turtles are solitary animals and because of this, they rarely communicate. They only communicate when it is time to start mating.

They use nonverbal communication by touching, squirting water, blinking, biting, and hissing.

DAILY LIFE

When not eating or sleeping, sea turtles are very active. They swim long distances.

They spend most of their time underwater but need air to survive so they hold their breath.

Every few hours, sea turtles go to the surface to breathe.

BEHAVIOR

During the first 3-5 years of life, sea turtles spend most of their time in the pelagic zone.

Once they are adults, sea turtles move closer to the shore.

Females will come ashore to lay their eggs on sandy beaches during the nesting season.

Did you know?

Sea turtles usually **migrate** over large distances. Some sea turtles swim more than 10,000 miles (16,000 kilometers) a year between nesting!

FAMILY LIFE

They dig a hole 16-20 in (40-50 cm) deep and fill it with a clutch of soft-shelled eggs. A clutch (group of eggs) can have anywhere from 50 to 350 eggs! They cover the eggs with sand and vegetation to hide the nest. All this takes about 30-60 minutes.

After laying eggs, females returns to the ocean leaving the eggs alone. The eggs will incubate for 50-60 days.

Most species of sea turtles hatch at night.

The eggs in one nest hatch together over a short period.

Baby sea turtles are known as "hatchlings".

Cooler temperatures turn eggs into males.

Did you know?

Sand temperature is important in deciding if a baby sea turtle will be female or male.

Baby sea turtles ("hatchlings") break free of the egg shell, dig through the sand, and crawl into the sea.

Only 1 out of 1,000 hatchlings survives to be an adult. They have many natural predators such as birds, crabs, and fish. Larger hatchlings have a higher chance to survive because they are faster.

Did you know?

Some turtles make nests in large groups called "**arribadas**," Spanish for "arrival." Only the two ridley turtles, Kemp's ridley and the olive ridley, show this nesting behavior!

INTERESTING FACTS

1

Sea turtles CANNOT pull their head and flippers into their shells for protection, unlike many other turtles and tortoises.

Turtle hiding in shell

2

Some female sea turtles return to the very same beach where they hatched! This can happen every two to four years when they are able to mate.

Most sea turtles nest and hatch at NIGHT.

Kemp's ridleys are the only sea turtles that nest and hatch during the DAY.

This is more dangerous and less of them survive because there is a bigger change they will be seen by a predator!

4

When sleeping, sea turtles can stay underwater for 4–7 hours without breathing!

5

It was discovered that <u>hawksbill turtles</u> have biofluorescent properties. It means they can absorb sunlight and "glow" in the dark on rare occasions. It is the only known reptile that can do this!

6

Sea turtles have a symbiotic relationship with yellow tang. It eats algae growing on their shells.

LIFESPAN

Sea turtles live almost as long as humans. On average, they live around 50 years but can live even longer than 70 years!

Did you know?

One of the oldest known sea turtles is a green turtle named Myrtle. She can be found at the Cape Cod aquarium and is around 90 years old!

FUTURE OF SEA TURTLES

STATUS: endangered

Sea turtles have many predators but <u>human activity</u> is also very dangerous for them. It is illegal to hunt them in many countries but they are caught anyway.

They sometimes get caught in fish nets so they can't go to the surface to breathe and they drown.

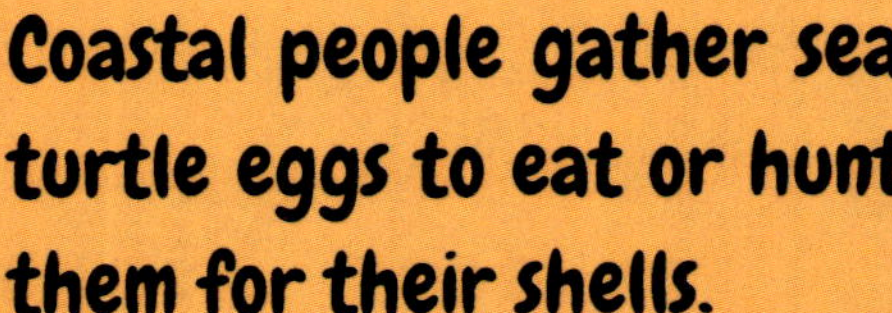

Coastal people gather sea turtle eggs to eat or hunt them for their shells.

Beach development is also a problem because of light and plastic pollution.

CONSERVATION

Conservation: the goal is to **PROTECT** sea turtles from threats such as illegal hunting and pollution.

WHAT CAN YOU DO?

Remember to always throw trash **INTO** a trash bin and **NOT** into the sea or leave it on the beach.

If you see a sign like this: **TURTLE NEST**, be careful. There are sea turtle eggs inside getting ready to hatch!

QUIZ TIME!

1.How many species of sea turtles exist?
a) five
b) six
c) seven
d) eight

2. Which sea turtle is the largest?
a) green sea turtle
b) leatherback sea turtle
c) flatback sea turtle
d) loggerhead sea turtle

3. What are baby sea turtles called?
a) cubs
b) calves
c) nestlings
d) hatchlings

4. How long before sea turtle eggs are ready to hatch?
a) 50-60 days
b) 120 days
c) half a year
d) nine months

5. What is called a clutch?
a) a sea turtle nest
b) a baby sea turtle
c) a group of sea turtle eggs
d) a mother sea turtle

6. Where do sea turtles NOT live?
a) in tropical waters
b) in open sea
c) in polar regions
d) near the coast

7. Why do sea turtles need to come to the surface?
a) to breathe
b) to warm up
c) to find food
d) to see where they are going

8. What helps sea turtles swim?
a) feet
b) flippers
c) lungs
d) shell

9. How long can sea turtles live?
a) 20 years
b) 50 years
c) 70 years
d) more than 70 years

Bonus question:

10. What is a sea turtle's shell mostly made of?
a) skin
b) scales
c) feathers
d) bones

Did you finish the quiz?
Well done!

Don't worry if you didn't know the answer to all of the questions at first.

You can go back and read through the book again to find the missing answers.

Hopefully you had fun reading and learned some new amazing facts about your favourite animal.

P.S.
Just in case you didn't manage to find all the answers in the end, we put them here for you to look up.
ANSWERS: 1.c), 2.b), 3.d), 4.a), 5.c), 6.c), 7.a), 8.b), 9.d), 10.d)

GLOSSARY

arribadas: large groups of sea turtles making nests

biofluorescent: when something is fluorescent, it can "glow" or give off light. BIOfluorescent means that a living being can produce light in this way ("bio" means life)

clutch: a group of sea turtle eggs in the same nest

conservation: protection of natural resources, such as soil, water, or forests, from loss, pollution, or waste

endangered: in danger of becoming extinct. When an animal is endangered, it means that few of those animals exist now, and it is possible that there will be no more of them in the future

flipper: a wide, flat limb on a whale, turtle, or other animal that is used for swimming

habitat: the natural environment of an animal or plant

hatchling: a young animal, such as a bird, reptile, or fish that comes from an egg

herbivore: type of animal that mostly eats plants

incubate: to keep warm until time to hatch

mating: a male and female of the same animal coming together to make babies

migrate: to travel a long distance to find a new habitat

nesting season: period of year when animals make nests and lay eggs

nonverbal: without speaking

omnivore: type of animal that eats plants AND animals

pelagic zone: part of the sea that is far away from land (open sea)

pollution: poisons, wastes, or other materials that cause harm to the environment

predator: an animal that hunts other animals for food

reptiles: animals that are cold-blooded, lay eggs, and have scaly skin

solitary: being, traveling, or living without others; alone

species (of animals): a group of animals that can come together to make babies with each other, but not with animals of other groups (species)

symbiotic relationship: a close relationship between two living beings close to each other or physically connected

terrestrial: living on or in the ground

turtles: reptiles with a soft body covered by a hard shell

Congratulations!

You have come to the end of this book.

Thank you for reading this far. Here is an extra photo just for you!

Leave us a review on Amazon if you liked the book!

Made in the USA
Monee, IL
19 January 2023

25697154R00026